AMAZING
SCIENCE

Nature's Fireworks

A Book About Lightning

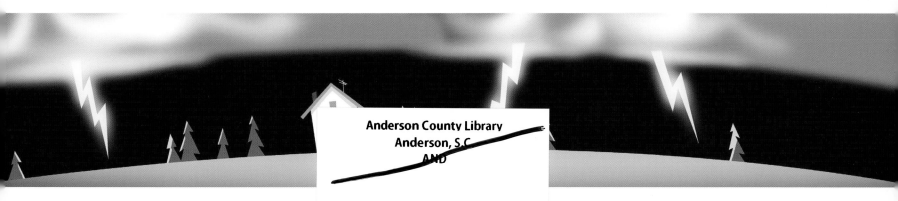

Anderson County Library
Anderson, S.C
AND

by Josepha Sherman   illustrated by Omarr Wesley

Thanks to our advisers for their expertise, research, knowledge, and advice:

Mark W. Seeley, Ph.D., Professor of Meteorology and Climatology
Department of Soil, Water, and Climate
University of Minnesota, St. Paul

Mike Graf, M.A., Instructor of Child Development
Chico (California) State University

Susan Kesselring, M.A., Literacy Educator
Rosemount-Apple Valley-Eagan (Minnesota) School District

PICTURE WINDOW BOOKS
Minneapolis, Minnesota

Managing Editor: Bob Temple
Creative Director: Terri Foley
Editors: Sara E. Hoffmann, Michael Dahl
Editorial Adviser: Andrea Cascardi
Copy Editor: Laurie Kahn
Designer: Nathan Gassman
Page production: Picture Window Books
The illustrations in this book were rendered digitally.

Picture Window Books
151 Good Counsel Drive
P.O. Box 669
Mankato, MN 56002-0669
1-877-845-8392
www.picturewindowbooks.com

Printed in the United States of America.

Library of Congress Cataloging-in-Publication Data
Sherman, Josepha.
Nature's fireworks : a book about lightning / by Josepha Sherman ;
illustrated by Omarr Wesley. v. cm. — (Amazing science)
Includes bibliographical references and index.
Contents: Lightning begins—Lightning is electricity—
Thunder and lightning—How far lightning travels—
Forked and ribbon lightning—Sheet and heat lightning—
Lightning around the world.
ISBN 978-1-4048-0093-9 (hardcover)
ISBN 978-1-4048-0337-4 (paperback)
1. Lightning—Juvenile literature. [1. Lightning.]
I. Wesley, Omarr, ill. II. Title.
QC966.5 .S48 2003
551.56'32—dc21
                                                    2003004701

Table of Contents

Flash! Lightning streaks from a dark cloud. ***Crash!*** Thunder shakes our roofs and windows. A lightning storm dazzles the sky like flickering fireworks.

Lightning Begins

High above the ground, water droplets
and ice crystals swirl and swarm
inside the moving clouds.

The tiny particles bump into one another.
When the particles rush together,
they become charged. Electricity is created.

Lightning Is Electricity

A single stroke of lightning
carries millions of volts of electricity.
Each stroke heats the air in its path
to as much as 50,000 degrees Fahrenheit
(27,760 degrees Celsius).
That is five times as hot as
the surface of the sun.

9

Thunder and Lightning

The heat from lightning makes air expand quickly. Expanding air makes a **booming, bursting** sound like a firecracker. This is the sound of thunder.

Thunder and lightning happen at the same time.
Light travels faster than sound. This is why
we often see the flash before we hear the boom.

How Far Lightning Travels

Lightning can flash faster than you can blink. During a single flash, lightning can streak down to the ground and back up to the clouds. A lightning stroke that flashes down to earth can stretch up to nine miles (14 kilometers). That's taller than the world's highest mountain. Lightning that flashes from cloud to cloud can travel even longer distances.

Ribbon Lightning

Ribbon lightning darts from the sky.

It looks like jagged streaks side by side.

Forked Lightning

Forked lightning looks
like an upside-down tree.
The branches of electricity
reach through the clouds.

15

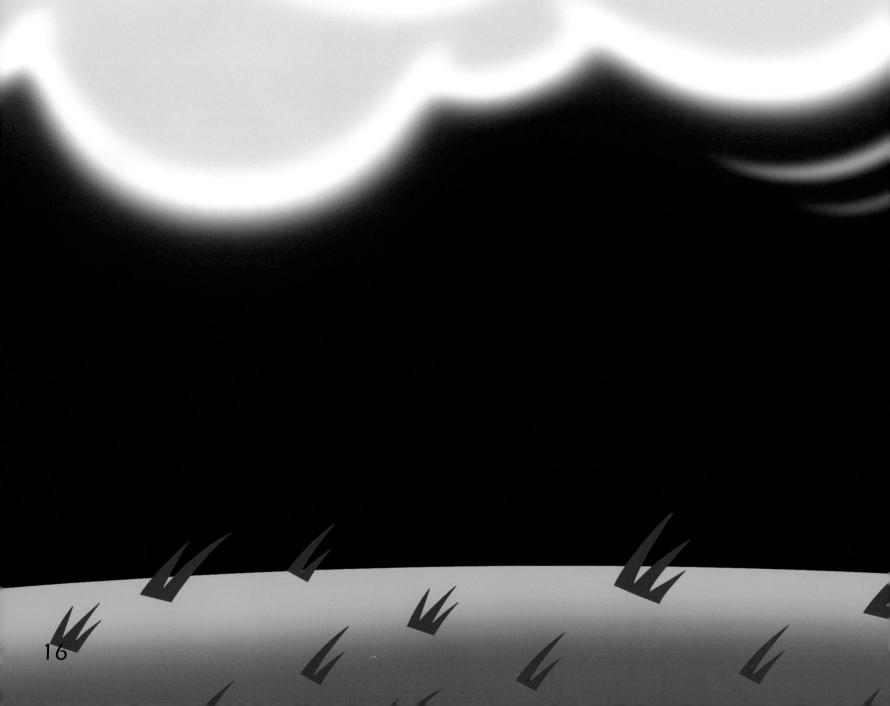

Sheet Lightning

Sheet lightning streaks inside a cloud.

The cloud lights up like a bright, white sheet.

16

Heat lightning happens during the hot summer. It looks like faraway flashes in the sky. Heat lightning is too far away for its thunder to be heard.

Lightning Around the World

Every day, lightning flashes from thousands of thunderstorms around the world. Every second, more than 100 lightning bolts hit the ground.

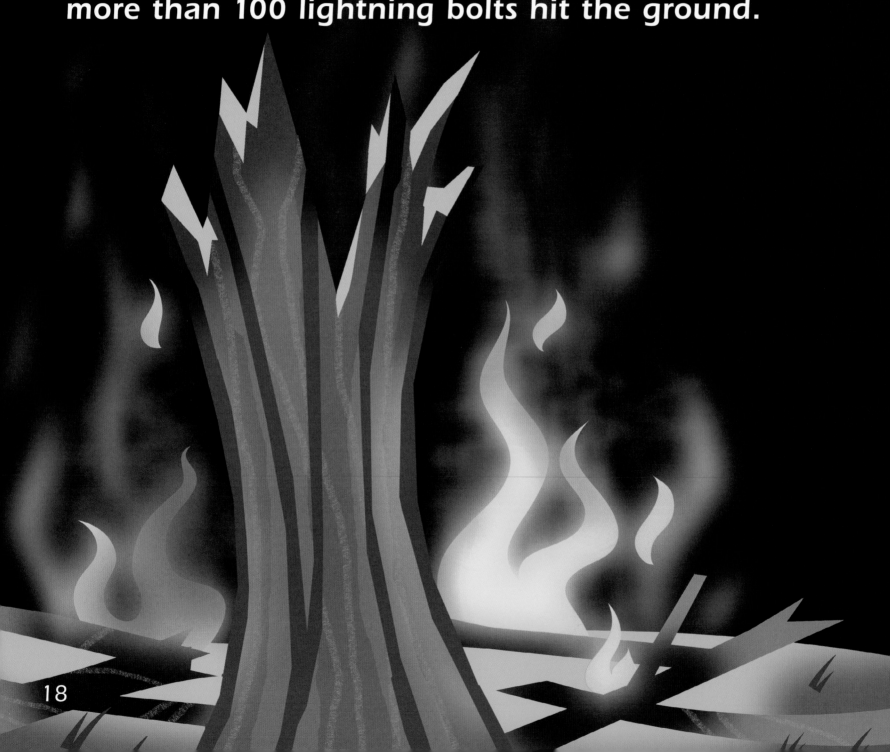

Lightning can strike a tree or dry grass.
When this happens, a wildfire can start.
Lightning bolts can hit tall buildings.
They also can hit electrical towers,
houses, and cars.

Flash! Lightning is streaking through the clouds.

Every flash is another display
of nature's fireworks.

You Can Make Lightning

What you need:

- a thumbtack
- an aluminum pie pan
- a pencil with a new eraser
- a foam plate
- a small piece of wool fabric

What you do:

1. Make sure you have an adult help you.

2. Push the thumbtack through the center of the aluminum pie pan from the bottom.

3. Push the eraser end of the pencil into the thumbtack. You have made a handle to lift the pan.

4. Place the foam plate upside down on a table. Rub the bottom of the plate with the wool for one minute. Ask an adult to time you. Be sure to rub the plate hard and fast.

5. Pick up the pan using the pencil, and place it on top of the upside-down plate. The bottom of the pan should be touching the bottom of the plate. Touch the pie pan with your finger. If you don't feel anything, try rubbing the plate again.

6. You also can try turning the lights out when you touch the pan. What do you see?

Fast Facts

- It does not have to be raining outside for lightning to strike. Lightning can strike both before and after the rain falls, or even when there is no rain at all.

- Lightning helps nature by putting nitrogen into the ground and air. Nitrogen is a nutrient. That means it feeds plants and helps them grow.

Safety Tips

- Windows, water faucets, pipes, telephones, and electrical outlets can be dangerous when there is lightning in the sky. You should not run water or talk on the phone if you see lightning. You could get an electrical shock.

- Benjamin Franklin once flew a kite in a lightning storm. That is how he learned about electricity. But today, we know lightning is very dangerous. If you see lightning, you should go indoors right away.

Glossary

expand—to get bigger

forked—split into two or more branches or points. The branches of a tree are forked.

particle—a very small piece of something, like a bit of ice

stroke—a sudden action or force

volt—a unit for measuring electricity

To Learn More

More Books to Read

Branley, Franklyn M. *Flash, Crash, Rumble, and Roll.* New York: HarperCollins, 1999.

Dussling, Jennifer. *Lightning: It's Electrifying.* New York: Grosset & Dunlap, 2002.

Saunders-Smith, Gail. *Lightning.* Mankato, Minn.: Pebble Books, 1998.

On the Web

FactHound offers a safe, fun way to find Web sites related to topics in this book. All of the sites on FactHound have been researched by our staff.

1. Visit *www.facthound.com*
2. Type in this special code: 140480093X.
3. Click on the FETCH IT button.

Your trusty FactHound will fetch the best sites for you!

Index